The *Ruins of* Summer

David Whitwell

 *redcliffe*

First published in 2017 by
Redcliffe Press Ltd.,
81g Pembroke Road, Bristol BS8 3EA

info@redcliffepress.co.uk
www.redcliffepress.co.uk

 @redcliffepress

 @redcliffepress

ISBN 978-1-911408-25-3

British Library Cataloguing in Publication Data
A catalogue record for this book is available from the British Library

Typeset in Hoefler 11/14
Design and typesetting www.stephen-morris.co.uk
Printed and bound by Short Run Press, Exeter

For Carolyn

Acknowledgements

Thanks are due to all the Lansdown Poets and especially to our leader Charles Thompson who has inspired us and kept us going.

I am very grateful to David Cook, Philip Lyons, and Matthew Barton for many years of patient encouragement. Without them the poems would not be here.

Jeremy Mulford was invaluable as a wise and long-suffering friend and editor. His enthusiasm was infectious and what he didn't know about writing, was not worth knowing. Sadly he died just after he finished working with me preparing these poems for publication.

Some of these poems have previously appeared in the three anthologies published by the Lansdown Poets in 2008, 2010 and 2012. The poem 'Barrow' won the Lisa Thomas Poetry Prize in 2015.

Contents

Escape Plan

Sometimes it's as though you don't give a damn.
The house and all our little comforts
could be swept away, or carried off by a mob,
with us left running for the hills,
foraging for berries,
anything to keep alive.

It's as though all this stuff,
laid out here in the city,
is just slowing us down.

At IKEA they have little rooms
to show off their sofas and beds and cooking pots,
but you want to move in.
This is all we need you'd say,
as you try them out for size.
You're drawn in, as though you've done it all before,
in an earlier life,
fleeing some ancient pogrom.

But how the tribe has grown,
with children to be gathered in, and their children.
So we found the hidden valley
up beyond the road end.
It's time to lay in supplies
and fortify the gate.
And one of us should buy a gun.

Near Asiago

One year we stayed in Asiago,
that was the address, but our hotel
was way out in the countryside.
Empty, out of season, just us
and a lot of friendly waiters.
We tried the cross-country skiing –
but weren't much good.
In the woods we came on war graves, some British,
from an obscure battle in World War I.

Then one day it snowed so hard
we couldn't go out.
Stuck in the empty hotel
we sat next to the silent pool,
and watched the snow floating down,
covering the fields and the trees.
We read our books and the day passed –
in silence and contentment.

I was reading the life of Churchill,
which made me think of those men in the woods.
Freezing and dying out there,
not long before I was born,
in a place now forgotten:
a dreadful place, that much I know.

I want to remember that day,
sitting there as the light faded,
night held back by the brightness
of a transformed landscape.

Sheds

Retreats for those who'll go no further.
Paint coming off,
boards bleached by the sun:
buildings consciously avoiding the jealous eye.
Blending in,
reflecting back the dreams of their inhabitants.
There's nobody here, nothing to steal
– so don't bother.
Yet this is a subterfuge,
because here is something real,
a Robinson Crusoe escape –
celebrating the single heart,
the pleasures of the spirit.

For such a thing men and women leave home
and travel to the ends of the Earth,
only to find a different sort of rabble.
It was here, but hidden
by a broken rake and a cracked window pane.
Here with a cup of coffee in an old chair
and the sound of rain on the roof.
Birds in the trees, squirrels,
and then a fox sunning itself,
watching you,
and disappearing,
as silently as it came.

The Swallows of Jerez

That time we stayed with Justin,
the swallows were back in Jerez,
swooping over the houses,
calling as they passed high in the air.

In the evenings we sat in Plaza Rivero,
cool at last.
And we met Arve and his new wife
coming from their house in Calle Francos.

And we went to Seville,
and walked in the Alcázar.
But it's mainly the swallows I remember,
watching them on and on in the evenings,
swooping and skirling through the canyons of the old town.

Our Cat Nutmeg

For once I must consider our cat Nutmeg
for she is now my constant companion
yet quite indifferent – doesn't care
for she will bite and scratch me if I stroke her
for she has no manners
for at all times she takes me for her servant
I give her food but often she won't touch it
but turns away affronted by my offering
for though she has the softest fur
and is the sleekest and most beautiful of cats
she's not for me to stroke
yet still she wants affection
for when she chooses she
will sit upon my knee
and purr and look content
as long as I don't touch
for she's a stubborn beast
and she is always here
so if we want to visit foreign parts
she's a problem to be solved
and that's not easy
for few can cope with her unreasonable behaviour
for which reason I've often wished she was not here
but buried in the garden like her mother
but then I would be sad
and miss her arrogant demands
her insolent defiance of all rules
that should apply to household pets

as though she knows
that when she's gone

she will never be replaced
she'll be our last animal
last reminder of a golden age
for this alone I'm glad to have her company

for it's only once we pass this way

La Préférence

So La Pref has gone,
demolished to make way for a new hospital.
Along with the Poor Law,
where the old men looked out on the square
as they sat all day doing nothing.
And Marie Louise, the mental ward,
where the little French nurse used to steady my hand,
as I gave the alcoholics their fixes,
intravenous vitamins, last thing at night,
in their padded cells.

La Préférence, our island home.
Where Leonard sang about Suzanne
over and over,
as the sixties were coming to an end.
No more mess dinners,
with dressing up and too much drink,
and God help anyone who came in that night.

Now it's always summer on the Island,
half day, the sun high,
and the road clear to St Aubin
and the beaches in the West.

La Préférence was the house in Jersey where we lived for a year.

St Andrew's

I read a few graves each time I pass.
A Judge from Gibraltar, a General from Puna,
and a Surgeon from the Madras Native Infantry,
over there by the gate: he died so young.
Others you have to look for under the trees,
Mrs Ann Yearsley, the Bristol Poetess, and
Mary Barlow, faithful friend and servant
commemorated by *her bereaved and attached mistress*.

St Andrew's is gone, destroyed by enemy action in 1940.
So with no services and no priests,
the trees are a church, open to all,
a welcoming space of leaves and birdsong.
In high summer the lime walk is a wonder
a corridor of leaves, inhabited by squirrels,
which people stop and address and show to their children.

And sometimes there's someone sitting under the trees
and for days I see them, each time I pass
a western sadhu,
a penitent open to the sky –
enacting a life I can only dream of.

And in July the fireweed,
the same that blazed on bomb-sites years ago,
suddenly appears, hiding the ruins
under masses of pinky-red flowers.
Then as Remembrance Day approaches,
the ground sprouts little crosses
adorned with poppies.
And always every day they're passing through,

resting on benches that recall some who loved this place,
or walking slowly, wondering about logs
cut down last year and left here still,
or about those carved inscriptions,
harder to read each year.
And yet among the shattered relics
there is one modern stone, to my old neighbour,
so modest it simply says 'Remember Tim'
– which I do.

Resting Abroad

Took a budget airline down to Málaga,
to live a life
cut off from habitual ways.
No hablo español, you see,
I DON'T SPEAK SPANISH.
Talk in the marketplace – it's
a distant street-opera.
I'm not involved,
and not responsible.

Wandering in the sun with no particular destination,
these are calm days,
life seen from the outside.
For the library we have no use (can't read),
bookshops – the same.
So we rest our brains
in our sultry southern city,
idling in the heat of the afternoon,
then out in the evening, to sit in the square and
observe the Spanish,
guessing at what they mean.
Always enjoying the unfamiliar,
not risking the magic with too much knowledge.
Holding on to our outsider's view,
so easily ruined by contact with
the welcoming ex-pat English.

The Walking Life

This morning, frost on the grass,
the air freezing,
a dazzling yellow sun.
New life.

I've taken the books to Oxfam
and the journals
have gone to the tip.
There'll be no more studying.

We walk early and late.
At first it was a health thing
for the heart,
to keep the joints moving.
But now along cliffs, through woods,
over distant hillsides
stumbling and footsore,
it's become a way of life.
Hoping for the unexpected,
the chance encounter.
Then the miraculous recovery,
as we walk off into a new morning
to start all over again.

Culbone Woods

All night wind rattled the windows,
rain pummelled the glass
and in the grey of morning
we set off.

There were puddles on the path,
water dripping from the trees,
and the noise of a stream filled the valley –
loud, insistent, almost mechanical,
as if the old mill, now a woodman's cottage,
was back in business.

It was a steep broken coombe
the trees wrestled by the wind, almost blocking the sky,
beside the church at Culbone
where the lepers who lived in the woods
were allowed to watch the sacred rites
through one small chancel window.

Walking that morning above Porlock
I thought of Coleridge
and his story of a man who interrupted him.

Later, above the tree-line, we surprised
a group of wild horses
playing together,
fighting, charging across the moorland
and the day lifted,
brightness appeared over the sea
and light picked out the distant coast of Wales.

Sweet Thames

You'll find the steps going down
just below the Festival Hall.
And if you go there
when the tide is low,
you can walk upon the sand.
Children run and play,
and men with spades
look for things buried by the river.

Down there at the water's edge
the towers of the city rise up,
immense and magnificent,
while the stream, at your feet, flows past,
carrying everything out to sea.
It's been like this since the Romans
built their fort on the north bank.

Here you feel the sun on your face,
hear the gulls and distant children.
It's beyond the reach of the law.
They are running wild, and
people of all ages are stripping off,
drinking, smoking,
lying about just as they please.

We are down below the usual level:
below the shops and cafes
and all the unreal glitz of the city.
Here is a lower stratum, uncontaminated.
A place to reconnect with the bedrock,
rediscover firm ground.

The Ruins of Summer

I

Living beyond the road end, few people pass,
today nobody. The road empty.
The good road stops at the mountain gate.
Cottage by the gate deserted.
The old man too confused to live alone:
his family quarrel and resolve nothing.

Hot October and the air full of seeds
floating on light breezes.
The shelter keeps off the sun.
The valley stretches below –
far off a white farmhouse,
but here today it is silent.

It is the ruins of summer,
grass fallen down,
trees drab, but still green.
Seeds and fruit and decay advancing.
We are impatient for the storms and frost,
we take lightly the glory of the day,
we wish on the year,
but regret its passing.

II
Again in my lookout on the hill.
Sun hot on my face, this January day.
Still day, peaceful, quiet.
Below is a sea of fog
lapping at the lower reaches of this high valley.
But here such clear air, such blue sky –
looking out over the clouds,
like being in heaven.

Many things to do, but
I sit and look to the distance.
Nothing will come with time.
I save up uncompleted tasks
for another day.
Today I cultivate idleness,
my rarest attainment.
The conserving of hope and possibility.

Borderlands

This secret country is easily passed by,
not an obvious destination.
Quiet, secluded – a rolling countryside
of little towns and ancient farms
set among fields and woods.
It is the border where England meets Wales
along the banks of Wye and Monnow.
A country that in living memory, when no one was looking
became part of Wales.
There were no riots,
no one was killed.

This heartland lies there, dreaming on
through the days of summer.
So different from Gaza
where neighbours hate and fight and kill each other
under the blazing sun.
We hardly notice the peace and goodwill.
Yet this place had its day.
This sacred heartland of Wales-next-to-England

You see it if you look –
Welsh placenames surrounded by encroaching English,
the towns – planted here
– English settlements on ancient Welsh soil,
and every few miles – a massive castle
Usk, Skenfrith, the White Castle, Raglan
and many more on this front line
where people hated and fought for generations
but in the end
learned to live together,
mingled and married and settled
and were allowed to forget.

Voices on the Hill in Summer

Cutting grass in the field by the house,
isolated and surrounded
by the noise of my machine,
cut off from everything outside:
a special loneliness develops.
And as the day progresses I wonder –
Do I hear voices talking to me?
An argument that goes on and on.
And I'm not really listening,
but when I stop, the words continue
almost audible in the still air.

Looking down from the hill
towards the farms and fields
of the Usk Valley,
a sheltered landscape of green and shadow,
I see woodsmoke over the trees.
A thin blue column rising up –
hazy and indistinct.
An ancient signal,
someone is here in the woods.

Gwyn's Passing

Gone just a few years and already
the land is slipping away.
Bracken advancing more each year,
thistles uncut, and blackthorn spreading through the ground.
The fences cannot hold – mountain sheep break through,
and soon your land will be lost:
walls and fences hidden in a sea of green.
It will become like the lost acres on the mountain –
slowly returning to the scrubby woodland
that was here after the ice.

It began when they killed the sheep,
your rugged mountain flock.
Just a precaution, they said.
Nothing actually wrong with them,
but your neighbour had the plague,
so they all had to go.
The sheep were bad enough,
but it was the cattle,
killed as they stood in the yard by the house –
that was what did for you.
The stroke followed after.

So now, who will farm the waste?
What we took for natural order
a fine balance, was man-made
achieved by generations,
only to be swept away,
once its guardians depart.

Land Art

A mark on the ground is all it takes
to show I passed this way.
And sticks I piled in the wood,
in a simple wigwam shape,
may last a few years –
and perhaps someone will see
their slow decay.

The trees obscure brief works of man.
Imogen's camp fades into the leaf mould,
but if you go now,
there's still a trace of where they slept.

I wanted more –
something to remain after us.
A stone circle
hidden in the wilderness
might last a thousand years.
Such folly,
where will it end?

I will copy Richard Long,
my wandering landscape hero.
Take a clear still day
and sit beside the pond,
and with a finger
draw on the face of the water.
Draw an eye looking up at the sky.

Things Fall Apart

Heat haze in a summer field,
filled with flowers of meadowsweet –
air heavy with scent.
The ground squelches,
steaming after rain.

The woods bursting out with new leaf,
press in on all sides –
a million shades of green.
Birds are hidden, but song fills the air,
mixing with the sound of bees.
Through it all a stream is heard.

The calm broken by a rock
loosed from the cliffs above, crashing down,
bouncing high as a man's head,
clearing a path through the wilderness.
Then silence: until the next time.

The mountains are falling –
something a young man might hardly notice:
– just a rock falling in a wood,
nothing in the wider scheme of things.
And if no one heard it – would it matter?
An academic question.
And whatever the answer,
rocks continue to fall,
will always fall.
Slowly, imperceptibly,
the Earth unwinds.

On the Blorenge

To give it a name
it's Millstone Grit.
It's hard and heavy,
granular and grey.
Strewn across the hillside,
walls stretching up into the heather.
Massive walls,
ramparts against the rain,
built at such cost.
Now abandoned,
lost in a sea of bracken.

There are tracks all over
made by the sheep.
Easy to see in winter,
but in summer
when the fern's as high as a man's head,
there's no way through.
And if you get lost
on the hills as darkness falls,
there are old mine workings
to think about.
And on that featureless convexity of hill
where even the sheep are lost,
you'll need the stars to guide you.
Up here where the moon is a searchlight
and the stars retain
their ancient brightness.

Deep in the Country

Choosing time alone,
up in the hills away from people,
as though all you want is yourself
and your own private world –
but it's not like that.

Those days under the trees,
feeling the wind,
waiting for rain,
create a heightened attentiveness.

As time passes
the mind moves outside itself
producing a kind of solitude
that is not inward looking.

Silence all around
leads to growing silence within.
The old arguments are replaced
by unexpected encounters.
Noises in the woods
or mist rising like smoke from the valley below.

Almost by accident
you learn to be free of thought.
You forget you are there,
a stone in the wilderness.

Child of the Fifties

Walking back from school
I liked to stop in the village
and watch the blacksmith
hammer the red iron,
hear the hiss and smell the burn
as he nailed it to the horse's hoof.

I'd press my face to the glass
at the village shop, and ask
what she had for one penny:
then walking on sucking sweets
I'd trail along the lane or through the fields,
idling my way home.

No, you'll never believe all that,
nor that I was happy
and the sun shone all summer long.
If only I had proof.
Memory is such a fraud and
tells us such terrible lies.

Old Mrs Naylor is no more,
and her shop
with its stale food and smell of mouse
is long gone.
But of the sweets I do have evidence:
they rotted my teeth, and the holes remain
to this day.

A Wonderful Day

As the days pass
you may come to understand
that something different from what you expected
is always possible.

There's no hurry now,
nowhere to go and no one to see.
This is the time and the place we were all looking for.

Remember that time you walked the dog
on the shore one afternoon
with the tide low and the wind rattling the rigging
of boats pulled up on the sand.
You had to dodge the rain by sheltering in the boathouse
then as the sun came out
you walked on across the fields,
and the dog went crazy rolling in something nasty.
Remember it was just a walk,
it was one afternoon.
And when you got back to the house I was there.
I saw you coming up the drive,
heard the dog barking and you shouting.
It was a wonderful day.

Are there some things that I've forgotten?
Was it always going to end like this?

Sweet Red Apples

Yesterday I was trying to work,
but kept thinking about the orchard –
the one we had when I was a boy.
There was an old wooden shed
with a table and a chair,
and a window looking out at the trees.
One summer I sat there for days on end
reading philosophy
– while the apples ripened on the trees.
And it was good, even though
the reading was hard –
terrible dried up stuff.

The shed was old and dry
and gave off a wholesome woody smell.
The trees were weighed down
and the grass high
and blue with forget-me-nots.
And when my friends came they laughed
because I was reading Bertrand Russell.
We ate the sweet red apples
and went down to the shore
where we walked on the sand
and threw stones into the waves.
I can't remember the philosophy
or why I wanted to read it.
It's the orchard I recall
and going down to the beach
and feeling free
and having so much time.

The Photo

A man stands in the sea
in shorts and a many-coloured jacket,
up to his ankles in crystal clear water,
looking towards a horizon
that's hazy and indistinct.
He's turning away so we can't see his face,
or see what he's thinking.
That's all – there's nothing else.

I found it after he died,
left as if by accident at the bottom of a box.
But what if he picked it out,
and it does mean something?
The sea draws us in, but it gives back nothing;
nothing but grief.

Maybe it was not that at all.
Maybe he was laughing. About to turn
and throw something – a stone or
a dead jellyfish from the shoreline
and tell Hans (who must have taken the picture)
that it was too cold for swimming
and they ought to go for a drink.

Beachcombing

I was a beachcomber once,
spent days walking the Dee estuary,
alway hoping to find something.
There were dead birds,
some with rings on their legs –
must have been trapped, handled, noted,
then killed in a storm at sea.
Lots of stinking seaweed,
fish and crabs,
and unpleasant human rubbish.

Absorbed in my strange pastime,
which took me miles from home along the lonely shore,
I had a sudden shock.

Half-sunk in the sand,
shoulders turned away,
there was a torso, lying on its side.
And as I looked I saw the fishy tail
and female shape
of a mermaid lying at my feet.

That's what I saw, and staggered back
brought to my senses
by something that could not be –
but that first image is with me still.

It was a dead seal.

Nelson and the Bear

Things he did amazed us.
He could sit stock still
then jump up like a jack in a box
and run off across the sand,
turning cart-wheels and walking on his hands.
Do it again, we'd say,
and he'd grin and race off,
his bony body spinning round.
Such tricks.
And he knew so much –
long complicated words and
strange stories, still remembered after all this time.

Like his famous Nelson story.
How as a boy the famous admiral went to the Arctic
and nearly killed a polar bear.
His picture showed the little cabin boy
and the great big bear.
An image that came to the surface
in the clear-out, after he died.
All coming back now,
because another Horatio went to the same place,
met another bear,
and did not survive.

Horatio Chapple was killed by a polar bear in Spitsbergen 5 August 2011, the same place
where Nelson met his bear in 1773.

Cooper and the Doc

The War was all around us, but hidden now.
In the attic we played with a revolver,
he'd taken from a dead Belgian, and
a German bayonet, he'd picked up somewhere.
And there were boxes of medical supplies,
provided by the Red Cross,
so good for playing shops.
None of it ever explained,
this thing that was ending, just as we began.

I found that the Doc
had cleared out the attic before he died.
The gun handed in, and
all his loving letters,
sent to a young wife from the ends of the Earth,
must have gone up in the fires he had
in the orchard, that last autumn.

So I turned to Cooper,
living on, by himself, in the country,
pinned him down, said 'you must tell me'
and he was glad, shed real tears.
He'd always thought no one was interested –
the camp at Ocean Springs in the Deep South,
training up the raw recruits,
preparing for the War at Sea.
How when a man broke his arm,

he needed an M.O.,
and that was how they met.
And they hit it off and teamed up,
with wild nights in New Orleans
before they went to sea.
Cooper's moment came at the end.
Sailing into Sete he liberated the town,
then stayed on as governor,
ruling the French with power of life and death.
Years later they brought him back
and feted him and Margaret at the Town Hall –
but even then he never told his sons the real story.
Just as the Doc never described his days
getting the wounded back
from the beaches at Dunkirk.

Cooper came back to an office in Liverpool –
'Van Oppen, Importing and Exporting'.
He and the Doc kept in touch.
meeting each month at the Welsh Harp,
down on the marshes, looking out at the sea.
But the women they married did not get on;
their families never knew each other,
and their story was never told.
And now they've gone.

Silence

If the warrior does not come back,
and the sailor never
returns from the sea,
but is utterly lost, though
waited for anxiously in dreams,
then the message is lost,
and the son must comfort the widow
and the daughter stay by her.
And stories will fill the space,
making up what was never said,
inventing myths to live by.

But what if he returns,
and he's there in the evening
looking into the flames
but saying nothing?
And life goes on,
and it's empty,
and years pass and not knowing
becomes a poison and the silence
a kind of death.

Rodmell

In a pile of old sketches I found in your room
was one I liked and had framed.
It's been on my wall for 20 years –
it looks a special place,
a pavilion with high windows, set on a hill.
Written at the bottom: Hill Top, Mill Lane, Rodmell.

I know you went there several times and spoke of
the light and the curve of the hills.
I never joined you, but I've lived with it now,
that place you never took me.

Parking by the pub I walked up
and found the place hidden by trees.
Through a gap I saw those windows,
which now I realise
look out across the Downs
all the way to Peacehaven and the sea.

As I walked back it came to me
that this was the village where a woman put stones in her pockets
and walked into the river.

And I thought of that last summer,
how you lay downstairs
quietly watching your beloved river –
the tides, the clouds and the Welsh hills coming and going
and waiting, not wanting bothersome treatments,
because you knew that what you'd always feared
had finally come
and you were there to greet it.

Like the Sea

As we walked over flint and chalk,
high on the Salisbury Plain,
the wind ripped across the fields,
waves breaking and twisting.

Look, she said, holding me close,
It's like the sea:
I could watch this for ever.

She came from the sea,
she was an *Island Girl*,
and loved it all her life.

Years later the farmer planted wheat
in the field behind our house,
and she caught its movement in a painting
– I have it still.
She is long gone,
and the house is no more.

This thing with the wheat,
for which there is no name,
I saw it again last summer,
on the cliffs at Mothecombe.
Again, in the sun and the wind,
I had to stand and watch.

The Manxman

I knew a Manxman once
who though happy enough in London,
was always loyal to a call
that no one else could hear.

In his mind he had an upland farm
and there he'd take me
when the meal was over
and the wine far gone.

It's on the mountainside, he'd say,
up above Ballaugh,
surely you remember;
beyond the ruined houses in Glen Dhoo.

He said he'd change his life,
leave accountancy behind
and reclaim for the plough
land untouched since World War I.

The story deepened as night wore on.
A widow, living now a dull suburban life,
was sure to join him if he asked –
they'd been so close, in Ramsey, years ago.

Many evenings we visited
this Island of his dreams;
he was my cousin
and he passed it on to me.

They were always there,
the wasted acres waiting for the plough,
the cotton-grass bobbing in the mist.
And even though he never made it back,
he never quite gave up the hope he had.

Looking for TE Brown

My grandfather died before I was born,
but stories, and a few books
came down to me.
There were novels by Conrad,
and lots of Manx poems
I couldn't get on with at all.
I was told the old man liked them.
He was a sailor from the Island,
and could recite the dialect poems.

TE Brown seemed so distant,
a Victorian schoolmaster in a suit,
but since I ended up in Clifton,
where he'd spent his exiled life,
I had to have another look.

He wrote of the island he loved,
but he left and went away,
living more and more
in the island of his mind.

I looked for the famous poet
in Redland Green Churchyard.
Fighting through the brambles,
growing thick as trees
round that neglected plot.

He's lost and forgotten now,
the great Manx poet.
So I sat in the sun and celebrated
that all things pass.

May Hill

You keep saying how fast time is passing
and I keep agreeing with you.
So then as a test case
I ask about that hotel
where we stayed in Cornwall,
the one with the friendly waiter
who forgot to bring our food.
When do you think that was?

The question defeats us,
but I have a diary – it was Sennen Cove
and we were there three weeks ago.

Speeding time is a mad motorcyclist
roaring down the mountain road
on open day at the Manx TT.
By the time you turn your head
he's careered out of sight
leaving your ears shattered
your head spinning
and a wonderful smell of burnt oil
– the smell that carries me back
to May Hill in Ramsey in the '50s.

Unadopted

Unadopted and facing the south west,
the lane became a lake – all winter long.
No one could pass.
Yet the residents liked it that way.
It kept out cars
and door-to-door salesmen
and people like that.

As they became old, cut off by deep puddles,
how would they manage?
The cleaning lady gave up – couldn't take the road, she said.
The gardener kept going, but the council got him –
he was on the fiddle and had to stop.

They were on their own,
it was time to move – somewhere more sensible,
more appropriate for their time of life.
Everyone agreed, but they loved their house,
with its garden and views of the river.
The debate went on, but they still didn't move.
They looked at places – but hated them.
They were too small, had no views,
and worst of all there was nowhere for the dog.
Looking at unsuitable houses became a hobby.
They waited, and while still waiting,
health failed – first for one then for the other.
So they never moved.

As Things Change

I collect odd phrases I find lying about:
Snippets that might come in useful.
I store them on my laptop
to return to, another day.
It's so easy, this new world.

Hard to believe my mother never saw a computer:
and my father, right to the end,
expected that one day
the Soviets would come.

Today wiped clean, eaten by the computer:
all my precious words lost for ever.
So it's back to pen and paper.

As things change, so they stay the same.
And as for the Russians,
we'd better not forget about them.

Frog

I used to live next
to the British Museum
and every day I'd wander through,
so I knew every room.
I knew where crowds gathered –
how people love the mummies,
which I find very unpleasant,
and form a queue at the Elgin Marbles –
which are overrated
and of dubious provenance.
I like the Assyrian reliefs,
with their people and animals
and the ordinary lives of ancient kings.
And Sutton Hoo is quite extraordinary
and it wasn't stolen from anybody
but made right here.

But what I like best,
what I return to every time,
is a little stone frog –
carved from green marble
7,000 years ago, in Egypt.

Venice

I too have been to Venice,
Seen it in the morning,
walked till my feet ached.

I was just a child
and took away a secret.
It gave me something –
I thought was mine alone.

Just by being there,
was enough.
I didn't envy the natives,
I had become one of them.

But now I stay away
from all those special places.
There's nothing to be found,
it's just 'visitor experience'.

I'd rather walk along this path,
with many miles to go,
and no particular place
we're heading for.

The Fortunate Isles

And then we came by night
to the Fortunate Isles.
Not by careful navigation
nor yet by chance alone.
For we had made a choice,
surrendered to the sea
and let the currents
take us,
washing us away
from all the world we knew.

For we were young
and unprepared
for such a place.
They took us in
and cleaned our wounds.
Many days we lay there:
then rising ourselves
we took the cliff path,
right to the sea's mouth
and the end of land.
All this, many years ago.

Dreaming the Scholar Gipsy

Walking the Thames Path out beyond Godstow,
I follow the directions that I know so well
from Arnold's old romance.
But so much has changed.

The Oxford bypass dominates,
and roaring traffic never stops.
Hard to believe this is the *glittering Thames*,
haunt of *black wing'd swallows*.
But looking for the place
where men once went to swim,
I find the *abandon'd lasher*.
Lasher – local term for weir, or pool
into which the water falls.
Anyway, it's there, standing isolated in the fields
but only the foolish would swim there now.

Each year the river claims a few
victims of the undertow.
Cut off, lost, drifting down stream,
found days later:
annual cull of bright young men,
wasted, come to nothing,
just like the boy suicides that each year
shock and shame the city.

Where am I? Yes
walking on through the meadows.
I watch the livelong day,
people passing in the distance,
laughing, talking,

but too far off for me to hear.
They sit and then I see
they lie together in the grass
hidden among the buttercups
while I keep on my lonely watch
taking it in, and missing nothing,
waiting for a message,
a sign that things fall into place.
The sign he hoped would light his way.

But I grow bored and ill at ease,
it is not here, that's all. So
how did the Scholar pass his time?
And was he all alone
all through the summer days?
And what of the girls he passed,
the ones he gave the flowers on summer eves,
surely he wanted them?
And didn't he long for the old friends and
the feasting, and once again to enter
the *festal light in Christ Church hall?*
Summer evening at last grows dark, as
I re-cross the Godstow Bridge,
the water thundering underneath.
Back to the pub to have a drink
and the easy comfort of other people.

Why this stubborn fascination?
Why did he not just chuck it in
and give up his wait for
the Spark from Heaven which
when all's said and done
was never going to come?

The Green Girl

She came through the water meadows,
there beside the lazy river.
A summer frenzy was on.
I the impossible idealist
struck down by the heat of June
lay in the shade reading,
longing for something new;
but brain could not connect.
Idling, waiting for a world,
and there she was
each day as the sun went down.
She came riding her dappled horse,
hair down her back.
She saw me there and I saw her.

I'm never going to see my Green Girl again.
But if I turn my head there's something –
across the street or reflected off water.
The smell of cut grass
or resin from pine trees.
I'm dizzy with it,
open my mouth to draw it in,
there on the edge of a new world
I gulp and gasp but
always it escapes.

Penycloddiau

The green road ran on
high above the bracken
up to a barren moor,
reaching at last huge ramparts
From the summit a line of hill-forts
stretched out before us –
right to the edge of the known world.
The greatest of them was Penycloddiau.

From those hills and upland passes
we saw more distant mountains,
whose very names we doubted
were known by any at that time.

We didn't care,
lying there on bilberry bushes,
sheltered from wind by ancient walls.
Vapour trails high in the sky and
sky larks, almost out of sight,
singing on and on.

Fish

Fish, I thought he said fish.
Such a strange sound
came from his lips
as he answered my question.
A noise really,
like air escaping,
Fissssh.
Air escaping, yet how can
air escaping mean something.
A fish, a living thing
that lives in the sea,
or even a river.
Riverfish, is that the word?
Is that what it was,
a riverine fish?
River running whether able,
running anywhere,
down stream, streaming, out
out into the Milky Way,
thrown across the heavens.
Caught in the stellar wind
air escaping beyond reach
beyond, past caring,
past us and away,
always there
after we've gone.

From a Train Window

The edge of the woods –
a ragged no-man's land, lit
by the evening sun.
A man glances up and sees
a train passing.
Did he see me watching?
Before he turned on his heel and moved
back into the shade,
lost from sight among the trees.

What kind of life,
there in the woods?
Is it the Gypsy thing:
roaming at will, escape beyond
the metalled road?
Or was he merely passing,
on his way to something of no account –
just like me.

Old St Paul's

Old St Paul's is there,
just off the North Bridge,
down a maze of steps.
Open as promised,
morning service 8am.

Stepping into that ancient space,
there are echoes and a smell of pine trees.
This is high, high church: Scottish Episcopal.
And the trail of my pilgrimage ends here –
where Richard Holloway spent the years
struggling to believe,
surrounded by the beauty of this secret sanctuary.

Voices high in the chancel,
two priests, man and woman
dressed in green and purple.
And all around the space prepared,
but nobody here until they welcome me,
a non-believing foreigner.

Then they enact their mystery,
read the story of Abraham and Isaac,
joining themselves with generations past.
Voices rising and falling,
answers and refrains,
songs and poems.
They move together, raise their arms,
celebrating extraordinary things,
which may have happened,
so long ago.

Afterwards they smile at me,
pack up their things
and I set off, into the morning.
Memories in my head
of a different world.

Thought I'd Know by Now

Thought there'd be an answer,
thought I'd know by now.
It always seemed a lifetime
would be long enough:
but time passes and nothing comes.

I've seen it in pictures,
figures in a landscape.
Old men in tatters
screwing their eyes against the light,
staring far off to the hills,
speaking a language I don't understand.
And when it's translated
it's all about djinns and devils,
people flying in the air,
speaking to the dead
and living for ever more.
I've chased it all my life,
so many false starts,
the hopeful glimpse, the headlong chase,
mysteries from the edge.

And I reel back, 'Is this it?
Is this all there is?'
I might as well have stayed with the gipsy folk
wandering the green fields of old England.
Or Mme. Blavatsky dreaming up her crazy worlds
behind the veil.
And there's a catch;
it's only for those with faith,
others need not apply.

And the words signify something else,
the secret which is always a secret,
and will never be revealed.
And if you think you have it,
if you grasp a little bit
then you're wrong; it's somewhere else,
and somewhere you can not follow.

All that is possible and I will never know.
But what if it is here and now,
and the only mystery is this.
This place in the evening light
with autumn coming on
and the voices of other people close at hand.

Talisman

I first met Nietzsche in London in 1963.
He was living underground, passed on secretly
but nothing was explained.
He was a talisman:
a secret that would open doors
or windows into new worlds.
I liked his name, kept it close to my heart,
I have it still.
I was a late reader, had trouble spelling
which is why I hold onto words
and fill my house with books.

What he said is there for all,
a quarry from which great lumps of rock
are stolen by lesser men.
The doors and windows are open now
and I've read about him and his struggle.
How in Turin he embraced a horse and fell down
and was mute and stark mad until the day he died.

For me he was always a hidden pleasure,
meanings just out of reach,
but the hope changed everything.
It was never hard for me
to hear what he was saying,
but I don't do philosophy now.
I keep his words locked up,
and they're with me still.

This Theory

I have this theory,
I know you're not going to like it,
I've been working on it all my life.
Others have touched on it,
more than that they have stepped all over it,
shat on it.
Philosophers, many of them German.
The years I wasted thinking they had an answer,
but my theory hasn't changed.
It's getting closer now.

Something about reality –
there being a real world out there.
That's it – it only comes in snatches
sometimes we glimpse it
 – not beyond the world
or on a different plane
but here, right here where we live.

Others try to pass this on
but mostly they fail.
Just occasionally
something gets through.

Learning Not to Seek

For a student just starting out,
Bloomsbury seemed to lead
to a different world:
the Museum and its library,
bookshops smelling of incense,
and all those writers scratching away.

It brought back the legend of Great Uncle Dick –
how he gave up a glittering career,
withdrew to Sussex,
and wrote *The Gold of Dawn*,
and a dozen other unreadable books.

By chance, years later, stuck in Madras, (never a place for tourists),
I returned time and again to the Theosophical Gardens,
walked the beach at Adyar,
and explored the Temple of Theosophy,
                              / with its gross Victorian sculptures
of Mme. Blavatsky and Col. Olcott.
And as I rested under the banyan tree
(the same I'd seen in books years before),
I knew it all was folly.
Intoxicated with ideas,
but always lacking belief,
and what is a man without belief?

But maybe *Truth is a pathless land*,
as Krishnamurti the great 'World Teacher' said.
Raised to lead us all
he turned away the followers who called him Messiah,
saying... *be yourself*

don't have faith
believe nothing
don't follow anyone.
And above all...
learn not to seek.

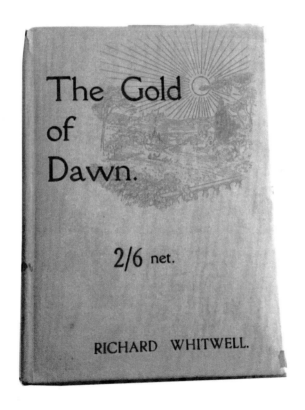

Ikigai

From the bar I watch him fishing,
a cormorant, here in the city docks.
Dipping his head, sudden jerky movements,
he disappears under the water,
but comes up without a fish.
He looks about, then tries again,
down, deep, out of sight –
gone so long, my attention wanders.
So many here, all busy doing nothing –
going nowhere.

In Japan they call it *ikigai* –
a sense that life does go somewhere,
that a purpose draws us forwards
through the darkest time.
But finding it – that's the thing.
A journey we may never start
or give up far too soon.

Then I see there are two of them,
he's got a mate.
They perch high up on an old chimney
standing, wings outstretched – drying in the sun,
living their lives
as though on a rock on a wild Atlantic coast.
Surviving here in the city.
While in the bar
we're going nowhere.

No ikigai.

Rothko

Dark on dark, maroon on black.
Deep dark reds and browns and grey,
oblongs, archways,
flat canvasses free of illusion.

That Rothko image,
recognisable from a hundred metres,
leaves us groping
for something beyond what is given.

The gallery irritates;
crowds of French school children,
disorientated tourists,
no place to rest.

We came because he was famous,
then mock his works,
belittle his adventures into the unknown.
Someone says
I could have done that,
many answer – *Amen*.

We expect too much.
That something will brush off,
something to set against our ordinary lives.
But it's not here.
Today in the gallery,
so easy and accessible,
the mystery remains hidden.

Kingfisher on the Roof

Kingfisher on the roof,
red sun behind palm trees,
then all the sky on fire
as darkness falls, 6.30 prompt.

Chilled Kingfisher
eases the tropical night.
Busses and cars honking on the road
motorbikes buzzing past,
and beyond, the trains,
real Indian trains, half a mile long,
lit up in the dark,
doors open, people sitting on the steps.

No news today, nothing from home.
No papers, no BBC,
hard to recall recent events
that seemed so important.

I thought of Lawrence on his 'savage pilgrimage',
a voluntary exile travelling the world.
Was it this?
Escaping the reach of the old life.
He must have sat
in the golden hour
as the sun went down.
He worshipped the sun; the true sun,
the one that has its back to us
and can't be seen from England.

And the message from my radio
– brought here to keep in touch...
not a whisper –
nothing from England
so the concerns from home
don't reach this far
and all that
living-in-the-head-trying-to-sort-it-all-out
doesn't seem to matter
up on the roof
with the Kingfisher
in the dark.

Tutitangel Mountain

A hill piled up with monstrous rocks,
granite boulders big as houses,
balancing, perched above the plain,
looking as though a single touch
would send them crashing down.
I cycled there on sandy paths,
sometimes just a muddy track
between the sparkling paddy fields.
The mountain still far off, I stopped
In shade beside an open well
And there I joined an ancient man
(probably not as old as me),
pouring water from a pot.
Greetings sir he hailed me
in English learnt in Punjab
many years before while
serving in the army there.

He fetched me water, swore it good,
and watched as I gave up
a golden rule of Indian travel
(never drink unboiled water).
Then, with lunghi back in place,
introduced his wife and son.

He'd lived close by for many years
and smiled to think I'd come so far
to climb this barren hill.
He happily showed me where to go
to reach the mountain foot
stranded there among the fertile fields.

Sure enough there was no path,
just giant rocks heaped up,
as I a midget clambered up,
through deadly thorns and spiny trees.
jumping rock to rock,
till at the highest point
I found a resting place
looking out across a level plain.

Ash

I stumbled at the threshold, startled by a beggar
with cleft lip and missing fingers.
Sweating with embarrassment, and the heat of the sun
                                    / in the courtyard.
I find shade in an alcove
where gods are decked in all their finery.
There on a bench, beneath a line of granite horses,
sits a school of dice players.
Lazing in the shade through the tropic afternoon.
They glance up as I pass
and a young man detaches himself,
signals me to follow, but I hold back,
afraid my presence will offend:
but I let him take me
because now I hear the music
and see the way that leads
to the heart of the temple.

It's hot and oppressive and difficult to breath,
faces lit by oil lamps, bright against the dark.
Drum beats and incense and such heat:
only the floor is cold and wet
He's still holding me, clutching my arm,
as I see the thing we are gathered around,
there in all its nakedness – the erect black phallus.
And I think of idols and the worship of idols,
and I draw back.

And there a young Brahmin, stripped to the waist,
pure black hair, and golden skin,
looking like a god himself,

a Greek god or Jesus figure
straight from an ancient mosaic.

He addresses each in turn, accepts their gifts
and offers them to Shiva, clothing the stone in silk,
presenting the bread and sweets and fruit.
Then breaking open a coconut
pours the milk over the stone,
down onto the floor where it wets our feet.

The holy man chants over each in turn
'til all the gifts are in.
Then he takes ash
moves round the circle marking each forehead.
And I am awkward, unsure,
ready to flee, but held there still.
Then the priest comes to me,
welcomes me, smiles in my face;
as though he always knew that I would come.
Then says in perfect English,
It is ash, to remind us what we are:
that we come from the mud and to that we return.
And then he marks me,
like the others.
And that is the end of it.
There is relief and smiles
as we turn to each other
and walk slowly back up the granite tunnel,
back into the light.

Night Thoughts

On the train to Katpadi
things were beginning to break down.
Air conditioning chilled us to the bone,
and we didn't know who would be there to meet us.

Philip Larkin frightens us with death –
real death, with nothing left behind,
– and no new life in another place.
So I look on this as preparing the way
and I'm grateful,
if it serves a purpose.

All the things we thought we want,
the effort we made and the time we spent –
maybe in the end, it comes to nothing.
Consider now the hardest truth –
that what we get
is what we always wanted.
All this while a deeper force,
working through the ground of every day,
delivered us to this point.
The thing that caught us in the end,
brought to nothing all our youthful plans,
was not some rare and vicious turn of fate,
an adversary hidden and unknown,
but our deeper will that in the end
must have its way.

So after this everything will stop.
Brain goes back to soil and
all we've done will be forgotten.

Carving stones might seem to slow this down,
stone being harder than human flesh.
But in the longer scheme of things
there's not much difference.

Is it fear of death that makes me sweat,
making it so impossible to sleep,
or that older mystery
covered up so long,
the fact that we were ever here at all?

KBO

Dead to the spirit of the age.
Struggling to adapt.
Never pretending
to know the score, or
what's expected.
Rejecting so much.
Clinging to the remnants
of totally undeserved privilege.
A master of the art
of accepting failure:
pretending what I get
is what I always wanted,
that the end-game
is where I wanted to be.
Carrying on regardless of cost.

Am I doing alright?

Barrow

The young doctor was amazed.
Did you really work at Barrow?
He looked at me, as though from another age,
and then we met a woman, brought in by the police,
and she knew me – you were at Barrow, she said.
And she smiled as though we'd shared something good,
even though on different sides.

I went back to Coombe Villa once
just for old time's sake,
trying to recall that far away feeling,
of a place apart.
But it was boarded up, the garden overgrown,
like a field coming right up to the windows,
and someone had scrawled across it,
Where have they gone?

I meet them still, in town,
and I know they're freer now.
No one keeps you in
a moment longer than required:
it's a human right.
They wouldn't go back for anything
to sitting there for weeks on end
waiting to be discharged.
But sometimes they tell me how much they miss it.
And I remember the slowness of it all,
we took such time.
It's a slow process, I used to say.
It was another age,
we did things differently then.

Help Me

I know I've got autism and look at my arms,
I keep cutting myself –
it took six stitches to stop the bleeding.
And I'm always running away –
like food and anorexia – it's an addiction.
I'm addicted to getting arrested.
Last time I was in the cells for four days:
that's against the law –
I could have them for that.
Now I'm afraid to go out,
I can't help myself – it'll be prison next time.
But that man, he always has a diagnosis –
personality disorder, bipolar disorder, whatever.
He wants me to take medication, and then
he says it's all up to me – because there's nothing wrong
– he must be mad.

It's not fair – I hate him.
Can you help me?
I need a new psychiatrist.

All We Do is Talk

Since you ask, I'll tell you,
Person Centred, that's what I am.
A follower of Carl Rogers
– heard him talk one time,
it was all the rage.
Genuineness, warmth, empathy
– just listening really.
I've done it all my life,
it's got me through.

I can see you've done alright,
but you can't feel my pain.
You may be listening
but I've seen you watch the clock.
I told you I was homeless
and you questioned me about it –
as though it was interesting.
All we do is talk.
Time passes
and already it's getting dark.
I told you I have no money
and you asked me if I have a social worker.
You'll be paid for this conversation,
I will have to beg.

At the Assessment

And this is Doctor W
and he is another psychiatrist,
so we have two psychiatrists here to talk to you –
How scary is that?
The social worker laughs, but
the man we have come to see does not seem to be listening.
And it makes me think,
what an odd thing this is.

I can listen – I'm good at that,
then ask a few questions
– it's expected,
then nod a bit,
and a point is soon reached
when I say I have nothing more to ask.

This man doesn't really answer.
He's talking to someone else, very quietly,
I think it's his aunt, who died two years ago
and left him like this –
in a world falling apart.
And his dog,
the poor dog will have to go to kennels.

Pills

If you stop the tablets too quickly
you will become unwell.
I used to tell people that,
but they thought it a ruse,
a trick to keep them hooked.
There are plenty who do that
I've heard them at it,
overwhelming people with science.
I never believed that stuff –
chemical imbalances in the brain.

I had a brain once,
my father gave me one, pickled in formalin:
I cut it up in the holidays.
He meant well, but I couldn't find my way
among all those pathways.

The brain is a mystery
and the pills are just meant to buck you up
or calm you down,
        so don't take too many, and
        be careful with them.

Enough of This

There's always Freud, hovering, pestering,
sitting there behind his desk,
surrounded by ancient curios –
gods, devils, emblems of powers
that somehow he's gathered to himself,
always telling his baleful stuff.
Insinuating,
hinting with a dirty smile, that
under the surface,
under our dull routines and harmless eccentricities
there are nasty things lurking
ready to jump out at us.

Well I've had enough of it.
It's just a story told to children
to make them fear the dark.

Joining the Group

The room is warm, light is dim
and the air hard to breath.
They nod as I come in, then go back
to their own space
while I struggle with chattering thoughts.
Like gnats, irritating and pointless.

Such a rush,
so many things left undone, and
my eye catches the angle of a roof
seen through the window
above the darkening gardens.

And I think about roofs and angles: slates and
Polish quarry workers.
I remember cutting slates and fixing them.
How I had to be very careful
not to fall off the roof.
But I didn't fall and I'm OK.
I shuffle my feet to prove the point
and someone looks at me, so I smile,
awkwardly.

Five minutes and I'm quieter now.
Outside is dark, the garden fades.
Inside at last I'm still,
the voices nearly stopped.
Now a soft feeling of wanting to stay,
to join the community and be included,
just for once
as one of them.

Breaking Us In

Herded like school children
we were silent and listened,
as they demonstrated the scalpel, and how to use it.
Little groups gathered round tables
where the objects of study lay before us.
Like children playing together,
we took turns and shared and helped each other out,
dissecting our bodies.

Was it just teaching as they said,
or a terrible game to break us in?
No one complained, except for the smell,
and that was not the rotting flesh but formalin,
scorching the nose and eyes,
impregnating the fingers.
It was on our clothes,
and little bits stuck to our shoes.

Off the dissecting room, there was another place
we didn't notice when we first arrived.
No one showed us but it wasn't locked.
Inviting, like a showroom or sweet shop
with shelves along the walls and
bottles of interesting little things.
But you couldn't see exactly what they were,
until it was too late
and you were up close
and caught your breath, groping about,
realising that this was also
something to be got through,
part of the course, part of what was to come.

Things with extra eyes or heads,
limbs or openings where none should be.
Creatures hardly human.
Who could put such things on open shelves?
Who would leave them there for us to see?
Yet with the sickness came a fascination,
made us look and brought us back again.

Staying Right Here

Calm in the morning light,
so much has changed.
I see my shadow,
like a dream that fades.

Not going on a journey but staying.
Not starting a new life but continuing.
Not finding a secret,
not even looking.
Being here again for another year,
and maybe another after that.
Not wanting to leave now
but knowing.
Passing mid-summer in a cooling world.

Just a few arrested at Stonehenge,
no real trouble.

And now no longer disappointed
by a cold summer.
After all these years the shadow speaks –
here we will stay.
I have pretended too long
that all this was leading somewhere:
that I knew a truth
that one day I would pass on.
Now I know
it is not so, and
it is a thing I celebrate.

Still Learning

Sounding like the thing you are
doesn't win many prizes.
Greyed by experience is not a story.
Wisdom, at such a cost,
taking such a long long time –
who wants it?

Yet still, amongst it all,
glimpses of something different.
The chance meeting that discombobulates.
Pulls away the comfy chair of easy prejudice
from under your fat bottom,
leaving you off balance.
Grateful for the friendly hand
of a smiling Somali man,
who's making the most
of hard times in a foreign land.

Things I Never Knew

Say something before it's too late,
time is short, so say it now.
Like: 'This is where I hid the key,' or
'Things that you've forgotten,
maybe there's still time.'

The sun is good today,
I never knew April could be like this.
Or another way to say it is –
'This is new to me.'
Always new things and
birdsong in the city gets louder, and
children's laughter carries on the wind.
Not forgetting we are children still,
amazed at what we see.
Landscapes always changing
so the world is new.

So many things I do not know.
Some cave-man logic fights against the change, and
something barely glimpsed crackles in the hearth,
and things beside the path, hardly noticed yet,
turn out different, far away from
anything we've seen before.

In the end we found a tree and cut it down,
then towed it home upon a sledge:
another day we will not see again.

Writing in Code

What you don't know, when you hear me read
about little insignificant things I choose to tell you
is that I write in code.

As I walked on Brandon Hill
a phrase stuck in my mind,
a devil tune, on and on, I hear it still.

If I tell you,
it'll infect you too.
Part of a collection of instances,
examples of what it's like being me.
Moments 1 hoard up
like delicious scraps of bacon
saved on my plate, when everything else is finished.
I won't tell you,
you don't need to know, and
anyway, it wouldn't mean anything.

What we share is a need to register.
To hold on to little bits of private world.
And I'm back walking on the shore,
heading out, away from the village
towards the river mouth.
The myths of youth
get stronger as time passes.

Cheerfulness Breaks Through

Sometimes all the grief in the world is not enough
and against all odds, cheerfulness breaks through.
– Leonard Cohen said that.

I thought of him as I walked past the hospital
– such an ugly building.
As though the man who built it said,
Nothing good will happen here.
I walked on, but it shouted after me –
Your time will come.
You will beg and wait in line
and smile at everything they say.

I know it well – the way it's done –
Tell me when it started.
What you noticed?
What kind of pain? How long's it been?

So they catch your suffering
with structured conversation.
It's one of those they say, *we know it well.*
And as they say these practised words they smile.
And you, left helpless,
hardly person now at all,
smile back and wait your turn.

For now I keep on walking,
but know it's waiting there –
the grey concrete waste of it.

I'll keep on going until they drag me in:
keep on fighting to the end –
hang on to something. But no I won't.
First sign of trouble, I'll be there,
demand they see me, do their tests.

All the things we know may fade,
and every comfort fall away,
and yet we find it hard to stop
the cheerfulness from breaking through.
Leonard Cohen said that.

Along the Way

Walking home by a different way,
not lost but off course,
on a street near the Lido that seemed familiar,
I met a man, a doctor I used to know.
So you come this way too, he said.
Are you prepared, shall we go inside?
And then he was gone and a wind came.

Hard to recall these things, which happen
in the blink of an eye.
Faces from the past.

But that walk goes on. People say
you'll never regret the things you do,
it's the things you don't do
that haunt you.
Like that day on the street,
but it's hardly worth mentioning.

Now I often swim at the Lido,
and some days meet my old friend.
And I wonder was it him, that time so long ago,
but he doesn't know,
or if he does he doesn't say.

Song

and all the time I'm trying to make a story
add together this and this and this
but I know it won't convince
the world's not made in manageable chunks

I can't help singing to myself
here in the empty house while
time is running out
and I give up
all I know are these few things
    take them how you will

it's raining here
the year is moving on
like limestone washed by falling rain
caves are formed
new forms of life emerge
and bones are found years later
carried by the stream

in the end the hardest rock gives way

Welcoming Dark

one is the welcoming dark outside
two is the light that is there in the morning
three are the beats of hearts keeping time
four is the sun on the flooded moor

following rhythms of each year
meeting the change with celebration
fire is there at the end of winter
shoots pushing up through alluvial mud

five are the thoughts of a dying man
six are the notebooks he left in the attic
seven the hope for a love that survives
eight is the rock beneath us all

over the fields and far away
where will we be in another year

Sometimes

Sometimes I forget what wine tastes like,
what I remember is bitter and sour.
Then I drink a glass
and I'm back with Keats,
transported to the warm south.

Sometimes poetry seems dead,
nostalgia for an unreal world.
But then I read a poem
and each word strikes me through,
as though my eyes are newly open,
showing me things I never knew.

And then I look at you,
and as you smile
I know that this is real:
and our life together
will last for ever.

Come Away

Think of all the wasted years,
piled up like ...
out of date telephone directories –
full of people you no longer know.

Or maybe not.
Send them off to be recycled
so someone else can go through all the things
you no longer care to remember.

Come away, to an ale-house on the moors
with log fires burning in the grate,
where we can sit all day
and talk of journeys we might have made
and the books we didn't write.

Don't think of things you leave behind
but keep on going
to places you never dreamed
would find a place on your itinerary.

Some breakthrough happened
while you were sleeping late
and now the world is different.
Things almost fantastical
are here within your reach.

Illustrations